All About
Sound

by Melvin Berger
illustrated by Cynthia Fisher

SCHOLASTIC INC.
New York Toronto London Auckland Sydney

For Jake, with love
— M.B.

ISBN 0-590-46760-3

Text copyright © 1994 by Melvin H. and Gilda Berger Trust.
Illustrations copyright © 1994 by Scholastic Inc.
All rights reserved. Published by Scholastic Inc.

12 11 10 9 8 7 6 5 4   6 7 8 9/9

Printed in the U.S.A.   09

First Scholastic printing, April 1994

Shut a door.
Sing a song.
Drop a spoon.
Blow a whistle.
Recite a poem.

You can make lots and lots of different sounds.
But did you ever wonder about sound?
Why are some sounds loud and others soft?
Why are some sounds high and others low?

Here are a few things you can do to find out
all about sound.

DO IT YOURSELF

Make a Fork Ring

Hold a metal fork at the end of the handle.
Hit the prongs against a table edge.
Quickly bring the fork near your ear.
What do you hear?

You hear a ringing sound.
The sound is made by hitting the fork
against the table.

You can make other sounds by hitting one object against another.

- Clap your hands.
- Tap your feet.
- Hit your hand on a table.

What other things can you hit together to make a sound?

DO IT YOURSELF

Make Sandpaper Rasp

Find two pieces of sandpaper.
Rub them together.
What do you hear?

You hear the sandpaper rasping.
The sound is made by rubbing the two pieces of
sandpaper together.

You can make other sounds by rubbing one object against another.

- Rub your hands together.
- Scrape your shoe on the floor.
- Run a fingernail over the teeth of a comb.

What other things can you rub together to make a sound?

DO IT YOURSELF

Play a Rubber Band Guitar

Stretch a rubber band between your fingers
and *pluck* it.
Listen to the sound it makes.

Now stretch the rubber band even tighter.
Pluck it again.
You'll hear a different sound.
Try it with the rubber band looser and tighter.
Can you play a simple melody with your rubber
band guitar?

You can make other sounds by plucking.

- Pluck the bottom of a wire hanger.
- Pluck an elastic belt.
- Pluck the cuff of a sock.

What other things can you pluck to make a sound?

DO IT YOURSELF

Make Paper Quack Like a Duck

Cut two pieces of paper about 1 inch wide and
4 inches long.
Hold them slightly apart in front of your mouth.
Blow between the papers.
What do you hear?

You hear a noise that sounds like a
quacking duck.
You made the sound by blowing through
the papers.

You can make other sounds by blowing.

- Blow across the top of an empty soda bottle.
- Whistle through your lips.
- Blow through a straw into a glass of water.

Can you think of other ways of blowing to make a sound?

Hitting. Rubbing. Plucking. Blowing.
These are different ways of making sound.
But the sounds are all the same in one important way.
Each sound is made by an object shaking back
and forth very fast.
When an object shakes back and forth very fast,
it vibrates.

Sometimes you can see an object vibrating.
Sometimes you can't.
But you always can hear a vibrating object.
You hear the vibrations as sound.

All musical instruments produce their sounds
by vibrations.

You hit a drum with a drumstick.
Hitting the drum makes the drum head vibrate,
producing the sound of the drum.

The piano works the same way.
When you press a piano key, it moves a hammer inside the piano.
The hammer hits a metal string.
The string starts to vibrate, producing the sound of the piano.

To play the violin, you rub the bow across the violin string.
The moving bow makes the string vibrate.
The vibrating string produces the violin sound.

The guitar makes its sound when you pluck the
guitar strings.
You also pluck the strings of the harp to make
them vibrate.
Plucking strings makes them vibrate,
producing the sound of the guitar or harp.

Other instruments produce their sound by blowing.
Flutes, clarinets, and saxophones.
Trumpets, trombones, and tubas.
All these instruments produce sounds when you
blow into them.

Did you know that you also make the sound of your voice by blowing?

Inside your throat are two bands of tissue.
They are called vocal cords.
The vocal cords are in the larynx, or voice box.
When you blow air past your vocal cords they vibrate, producing the sound of your voice.

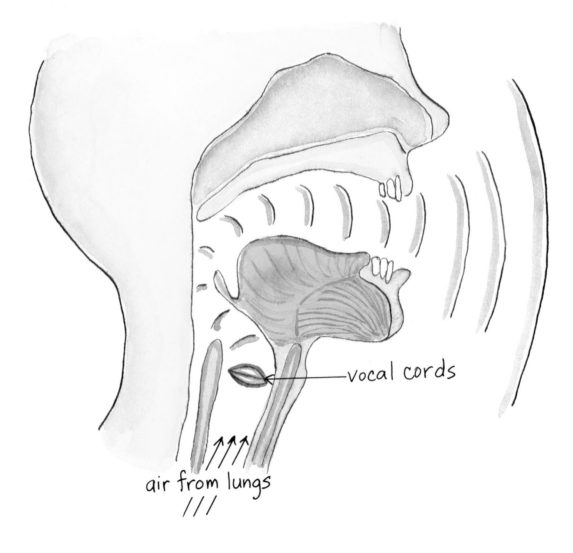

vocal cords

air from lungs

DO IT YOURSELF

Find Your Vocal Cords

Run two fingers lightly up and down the front
of your throat.
Do you feel a hard bump?
It is the front of your voice box.
The vocal cords are inside the voice box.

Rest your fingers on your voice box.
Now take a deep breath.
Say your name as you breathe out.

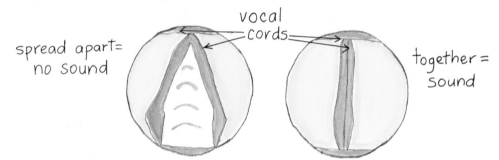

Do you feel a shaking inside your throat?
Your vocal cords are vibrating.
As they vibrate they make the sound of your voice.

What happens when you do not speak?
Your vocal cords are spread apart.
You can breathe in and out without making
them vibrate.
When nothing vibrates, there is no sound.

What happens when you want to speak?
Your vocal cords come together.
As you breathe out they vibrate.
They make the sound of your voice.

DO IT YOURSELF

Sing Up, Sing Down

Keep your fingers on your throat.
Sing up to the highest note you can reach.
Do you feel your voice box jump up?

Now sing down to a very low note.
Do you feel your voice box move down?

Sing from high to low a few times.
You'll feel your voice box move up and down.
You'll also feel a difference in the vibrations.
The vocal cords vibrate very fast for high notes.
They vibrate more slowly for low notes.

Try making different sounds.
Feel your voice box move.
Feel the different vibrations in your throat.

- Sing and talk.
- Shout and whisper.
- Squeak and growl.

Sounds can be loud or soft.
What is the loudest sound you ever heard?

- A jet plane taking off?
- Fireworks?
- A police car siren?

What is the softest sound you ever heard?

- A kitten purring?
- Someone walking on tiptoes?
- People quietly whispering to each other?

What makes loud and soft sounds?
To find out, all you need is a thin plastic ruler
and a flat table.

DO IT YOURSELF

Loud Sound, Soft Sound

Hold the ruler on the table.
Let half of it extend over the edge.
Hit the end of the table very hard.
Do you see the ruler vibrating back and forth
very widely?
Do you hear the loud sound?
Wide vibrations make loud sounds.
Now hold the ruler the same way.
But this time tap the end very lightly.
Do you see how the end hardly vibrates at all?
You'll hear a soft sound.
Narrow vibrations make soft sounds.

Sounds can also be high or low.
What is the highest sound you ever heard?

- A squeaky door?
- A flute playing high notes?
- Screeching car brakes?

What is the lowest sound you ever heard?

- The roar of thunder?
- A lion in the zoo?
- The tuba in a band?

What makes high and low sounds?
You can find out with the same ruler and table.

DO IT YOURSELF

High Sound, Low Sound

Hold the ruler with only 4 inches over the edge.
Hit the end that is off the table.
Watch how fast the end vibrates.
Listen to the note it produces.
The faster the vibrations, the higher the sound.

Now slide the ruler so 8 inches extend
over the edge.
Hit the end.
You'll see that the vibrations are slower now.
Also, the sound is lower.
The slower the vibrations, the lower the sound.

All sounds are made by an object vibrating.
The vibrating object sets the air around it
into vibration.
The vibrations spread out through the air
in all directions.
The vibrations are called sound waves.

You can't see the sound waves moving
through the air.
But they are there.

The sound waves strike your ears.
They make your eardrums vibrate.
Your ears send a message to your brain.
You hear the sound.
Anyone who is nearby hears it as well.

DO IT YOURSELF

Make Sound Waves

Stretch the rubber band once more.
Pluck it.
Watch the rubber band closely.
It looks blurry as it vibrates back and forth.

The vibrating rubber band makes the air vibrate.
The vibrations move out through the air as
sound waves.

You know that some sounds are very soft.
They are hard to hear.
But there are ways to make sounds louder.

Sending sound waves through a tube can make a sound louder.
The tube stops the sound waves from escaping into the air.
That's why doctors listen to your heart through a stethoscope.
The tube of the stethoscope makes your heartbeat sound louder.

DO IT YOURSELF

Make Your Own Stethoscope

The cardboard tube from a roll of paper towels or toilet tissue makes a good stethoscope.
Hold one end over a friend's heart.
Hold the other end to your ear.
Can you hear your friend's heartbeat?

You can use your stethoscope to hear other sounds.
Turn on the water.
Hold the stethoscope to the faucet.
You'll hear the water running.

Hold the stethoscope against a window.
You'll hear loud sounds from outdoors.

Hold the stethoscope against the refrigerator door.
You'll hear the refrigerator motor more clearly.

Try to find other ways to use your stethoscope.

Sending sound waves through something solid
can also make a sound louder.
That's why Native American hunters used to put
their ears to the ground.
They could hear running animals better
through the solid ground than through the air.

DO IT YOURSELF

Send Sound Through a Solid

Scratch your fingernail on a table.
The sound is not very loud.
Now hold your ear on the table and scratch again.
Is the sound softer or louder?

The sound is louder because sound waves travel
better through some solids than through the air.

Sound waves travel through wood.
They also travel through string.
You can try this.

DO IT YOURSELF

Make a String Telephone

Get two large, clean yogurt or cottage cheese
containers without covers.
Ask an adult to poke a small hole in the center
of each bottom.
Get a length of thin string.
Push one end of the string through the hole
in one container.
Tie a big knot.
Then push the other end of the string through
the hole in the other container.
Tie another knot.
Pull the string until the knots rest on the bottom
of each container.

Ask a friend to take one container and move
away until the string is tight.
You hold the other one.
Now ask the friend to place the open end of the
container to the ear without touching the string.
Speak softly into the open end of your container.
The sound waves move through the string.
Your friend hears your voice very clearly.

Now switch.
You hold the container to your ear.
Ask your friend to talk into the other container.
And you'll hear your friend's voice.

Now you know that:

- We make sounds when we hit, rub, pluck, or blow something.
- All sound comes from vibrations.
- Sounds can be loud or soft, high or low.
- Sound travels through the air and through solids.

Listen—and you'll hear a wonderful world of sound!